15

THE ZOO STORY

A Play

by

EDWARD ALBEE

D1149422

SAMUEL FRENCH

LONDON

NEW YORK TORONTO SYDNEY HOLLYWOOD

THE ZOO STORY

Produced at The Arts Theatre, London, on the 25th August 1960, with the following cast of characters:

(in the order of their appearance)

PETER   *Peter Sallis*

JERRY   *Kenneth Haigh*

Directed by HENRY KAPLAN

The action of the Play passes in Central Park, New York, on a Sunday afternoon in summer

Time—the present

THE ZOO STORY*

SCENE—*Central Park, New York, on a Sunday afternoon in summer.*

There are two park benches, one LC and one RC, facing the audience. Behind them: foliage, trees, sky.

When the CURTAIN *rises,* PETER *is seated on the bench RC, reading a book. He is in his early forties, neither fat nor gaunt, neither handsome nor homely. He wears tweeds, smokes a pipe and has horn-rimmed glasses. Although he is moving into middle-age, his dress and his manner would suggest a man younger. He stops reading, cleans his glasses then resumes reading.* JERRY *enters L and crosses to C. He is in his late thirties, not poorly dressed, but carelessly. What was once a trim and lightly muscled body has begun to go to fat; and while he is no longer handsome, it is evident that he once was. His fall from physical grace should not suggest debauchery; he has, to come closest to it, a great weariness.*

JERRY. I've been to the Zoo.

(PETER *does not notice*)

I said, "I've been to the Zoo." (*Loudly*) *Mister, I've been to the Zoo.*

PETER (*looking up*) Hm? What? I'm sorry, were you talking to me?

JERRY. I went to the Zoo, and then I walked until I came here. Have I been walking north?

PETER (*puzzled*) North? Why—I—I think so. Let me see . . .

JERRY (*pointing out front*) Is that Fifth Avenue?

PETER. Why yes; yes, it is.

JERRY. And what is that cross street there; that one, to the right?

PETER. That? Oh, that's Seventy-fourth Street.

JERRY. And the Zoo is around Sixty-fifth Street; so, I've been walking north.

---

* N.B. Paragraph 3 on page ii of this Acting Edition regarding photocopying and video-recording should be carefully read.

PETER (*anxious to get back to his reading*) Yes; it would seem so.

JERRY. Good old north.

PETER (*lightly; by reflex*) Ha, ha!

JERRY (*after a slight pause*) But not due north.

PETER. I—well, no, not due north; but we—call it north. It's northerly.

(JERRY *watches as* PETER, *anxious to dismiss him, prepares his pipe*)

JERRY. Well, boy; *you're* not going to get lung cancer, are you?

(PETER *looks up, a little annoyed, then smiles*)

PETER. No, sir. Not from this.

JERRY. No, sir. What you'll probably get is cancer of the mouth, and then you'll have to wear one of those things Freud wore after they took one whole side of his jaw away. What do they call those things?

PETER (*uncomfortable*) A prosthesis? (*He lights his pipe*)

JERRY. The very thing! A prosthesis. You're an educated man, aren't you? Are you a doctor?

PETER. Oh, no; no. I read about it somewhere; *Time* magazine, I think. (*He turns to his book*)

JERRY. Well, *Time* magazine isn't for blockheads.

PETER (*looking up*) No, I suppose not.

JERRY (*after a pause*) Boy, I'm glad that's Fifth Avenue there.

PETER (*vaguely*) Yes.

JERRY. I don't like the west side of the park much.

PETER. Oh? (*Slightly wary, but interested*) Why?

JERRY (*off-handedly*) I don't know.

PETER. Oh. (*He returns to his book*)

(JERRY *stands for a few seconds, looking at* PETER, *who finally looks up again, puzzled*)

JERRY. Do you mind if we talk?

PETER (*obviously minding*) Why—no, no.

JERRY. Yes, you do; you do.

(PETER *smiles, puts his book down, taps out his pipe and puts it in his pocket*)

PETER. No, really; I don't mind.

JERRY. Yes, you do.

PETER (*finally decided*) No; I don't mind at all, really.

JERRY. It's—it's a nice day.

(PETER *stares unnecessarily at the sky*)

PETER. Yes. Yes, it is; lovely.

JERRY. I've been to the Zoo.

PETER. Yes, I think you said so—didn't you?

JERRY. You'll read about it in the papers tomorrow, if you don't see it on your TV tonight. You have TV, haven't you?

PETER. Why, yes, we have two; one for the children.

JERRY. You're married!

PETER (*with pleased emphasis*) Why, certainly.

JERRY. It isn't a law, for God's sake.

PETER. No—no, of course not.

JERRY. And you have a wife.

PETER (*bewildered by the seeming lack of communication*) Yes.

JERRY. And you have children.

PETER. Yes; two.

JERRY. Boys?

PETER. No, girls—both girls.

JERRY. But you wanted boys.

PETER. Well—naturally, every man wants a son, but . . .

JERRY (*lightly mocking*) But that's the way the cookie crumbles?

PETER (*annoyed*) I wasn't going to say that.

JERRY. And you're not going to have any more kids, are you?

PETER (*a bit distantly*) No. No more. (*Then back, and irksome*) Why did you say that? How would you know about that?

JERRY. The way you cross your legs, perhaps; something in the voice. Or maybe I'm just guessing. Is it your wife?

PETER (*furiously*) That's none of your business! (*He pauses*) Do you understand?

(JERRY *nods*)

(*Quietly*) Well, you're right. We'll have no more children.

JERRY (*softly*) That *is* the way the cookie crumbles.

PETER (*forgiving*) Yes—I guess so.

JERRY. Well, now; what else?

PETER. What were you saying about the Zoo—that I'd read about it, or see . . . ?

JERRY. I'll tell you about it, soon. Do you mind if I ask you questions?

PETER. Oh, not really.

JERRY. I'll tell you why I do it; I don't talk to many people—except to say like: "Give me a beer," or "Where's the john?" or "What time does the picture go on?" or "Keep your hands to yourself, buddy." You know—things like that.

PETER. I must say I don't . . .

JERRY. But every once in a while I like to talk to somebody, really *talk*; like to get to know somebody, know all about him.

PETER (*lightly laughing; still a little uncomfortable*) And am I the guinea-pig for today?

JERRY. On a sun-drenched Sunday afternoon—like this? Who better than a nice married man with two daughters and—uh—a dog?

(PETER *shakes his head*)

No? Two dogs.

(PETER *shakes his head*)

Hm! No dogs?

(PETER *shakes his head, sadly*)

Oh, that's a shame. But you look like an animal man. *Cats?*

(PETER *nods ruefully*)

Cats! But, that can't be your idea. No, sir. Your wife and daughters?

(PETER *nods*)

Is there anything else I should know?

(PETER *has to clear his throat*)

PETER. There are—there are two parakeets. One—uh—one for each of my daughters.

JERRY. Birds.

PETER. My daughters keep them in a cage in their bedroom.

JERRY. Do they carry disease? The birds.

PETER. I don't believe so.

JERRY. That's too bad. If they did you could set them loose in the house and the cats could eat them and die, maybe.

(PETER *looks blank for a moment, then laughs*)

And what else? What do you do to support your enormous household?

PETER. I—uh—I have an executive position with a—a small publishing house. We—uh—we publish textbooks.

JERRY. That sounds nice; very nice. What do you make?

PETER (*still cheerful*) Now, look here . . . !

JERRY. Oh, come on.

PETER. Well, I make around eighteen thousand a year, but I don't carry more than forty dollars at any one time—in case you're a—a hold-up man—ha, ha, ha.

JERRY (*ignoring the above*) Where do you live?

(PETER *is reluctant to say*)

Oh, look; I'm not going to rob you, and I'm not going to kidnap your parakeets, your cats, or your daughters.

PETER (*too loudly*) I live between Lexington and Third Avenue, on Seventy-fourth Street.

JERRY. That wasn't so hard, was it?

PETER. I didn't mean to seem—uh—it's that you don't really carry on a conversation; you just ask questions. And I'm—I'm normally—uh—reticent. Why do you just stand there?

JERRY. I'll start walking around in a little while, and eventually I'll sit down. (*Recalling*) Wait until you see the expression on his face.

PETER. What? Whose face? Look here; is this something about the Zoo?

JERRY (*distantly*) The what?

PETER. The Zoo; the Zoo. Something about the Zoo.

JERRY. The Zoo.

PETER. You've mentioned it several times.

JERRY (*still distant, but returning abruptly*) The Zoo? Oh, yes; the Zoo. I was there before I came here. I told you that. Say, what's the dividing line between upper-middle-middle-class and lower-upper-middle-class?

PETER. My dear fellow, I . . .

JERRY. Don't "My dear fellow" me.

PETER (*unhappily*) Was I patronizing? I believe I was; I'm sorry. But, you see, your question about the classes bewildered me.

JERRY. And when you're bewildered you become patronizing?

PETER. I—I don't express myself too well sometimes. (*He attempts a joke on himself*) I'm in publishing, not writing.

JERRY (*amused; but not at the humour*) So be it. The truth *is: I* was being patronizing.

PETER. Oh, now; you needn't say that.

(*It is at this point that* JERRY *may begin to move about the stage with slowly increasing determination and authority, but pacing himself, so that the subsequent long speech about the dog comes at the high point of the arc*)

JERRY. All right. Who are you favourite writers? Baudelaire and J. P. Marquand?

PETER (*warily*) Well, I like a great many writers; I have a considerable—catholicity of taste, if I may say so. Those two men are fine, each in his way. (*Warming up*) Baudelaire, of course—uh—is by far the finer of the two, but Marquand has a place—in our—uh—national . . .

JERRY. Skip it!

PETER. I . . . Sorry.

JERRY. Do you know what I did before I went to the Zoo today? I walked all the way up Fifth Avenue from Washington Square; all the way.

PETER. Oh; you live in the Village? (*This seems to enlighten him*)

JERRY. No, I don't. I took the subway down to the Village so I could walk all the way up Fifth Avenue to the Zoo. It's one of those things a person has to do; sometimes a person has to go a very long distance out of his way to come back a short distance correctly.

PETER (*almost pouting*) Oh, I thought you lived in the Village.

JERRY. What were you trying to do? Make sense out of things? Bring order? The old pigeon-hole bit? Well, that's easy; I'll tell you. I live in a four-storey brown-stone rooming-house on the upper West Side between Colombus Avenue and Central Park West. I live on the top floor; rear; west. It's a laughably small room, and one of my walls is made of beaverboard; this beaverboard separates my room from another laughably small room, so I assume that the two rooms were once one room, a small room, but not necessarily laughable. The room beyond my beaver-board wall is occupied by a coloured queen who always keeps his door open; well, not always, but *always* when he's plucking his eyebrows, which he does with Buddhist concentration. This coloured queen has rotten teeth, which is rare, and he has a Japanese kimono, which is also pretty rare, and he wears this kimono to and from the john in the hall, which is pretty frequent. I mean, he goes to the john a lot. He never bothers me, and he never brings anyone up to his room. All he does is pluck his eyebrows, wear his kimono and go to the john. Now, the two front rooms on my floor are a little larger, I guess; but they're pretty small, too. There's a Puerto Rican family in one of them, a husband, a wife, and some kids; I don't know how many. These people entertain a lot. And in the other front room, there's somebody living there, but I don't know who it is. I've never seen who it is. Never. Never ever.

PETER (*embarrassed*) Why—why do you live there?

JERRY (*from a distance again*) I don't know.

PETER. It doesn't sound like a very nice place—where you live.

JERRY. Well, no; it isn't an apartment in the East

Seventies. But, then again, I don't have one wife, two daughters, two cats and two parakeets. What I do have, I have toilet articles, a few clothes, a hot-plate that I'm not supposed to have, a can opener—one that works with a key, you know; a knife, two forks and two spoons, one small, one large; three plates, a cup, a saucer, a drinking glass, two picture frames, both empty, eight or nine books, a pack of pornographic playing-cards, regular deck, an old Western Union typewriter that prints nothing but capital letters, and a small strong-box without a lock which has in it—what? Rocks! Some rocks—sea-rounded rocks I picked up on the beach when I was a kid. Under which—weighed down—are some letters—"please" letters—"Please why don't you do this?" and "Please when will you do that?" letters. And "when" letters, too. "When will you write?" "When will you come? When?" These letters are from more recent years.

(*There is a pause.* PETER *stares glumly at his shoes*)

PETER. About those two empty picture frames . . . ?

JERRY. I don't see why they need any explanation at all. Isn't it clear? I don't have pictures of anyone to put in them.

PETER. Your parents—perhaps—a girl friend . . .

JERRY. You're a very sweet man, and you're possessed of a truly enviable innocence. But good old mom and good old pop are dead—you know? I'm broken up about it, too —I mean, really. *But.* That particular vaudeville act is playing the closed circuit now, so I don't see how I can look at them, all neat and framed. Besides, or, rather, to be pointed about it, good old mom walked out on good old pop when I was ten and a half years old; she embarked on an adulterous turn of our Southern States—a journey of a year's duration—and her most constant companion— among others, among many others—was a Mr Barleycorn. At least, that's what good old pop told me after he went down—came back—brought her body north. We'd received the news between Christmas and New Year, you see, that good old mom had parted with the ghost in some dump in Alabama. And, without the ghost—she was less welcome.

I mean, what was she? A stiff—a northern stiff. At any rate, good old pop celebrated the New Year for an even two weeks and then slapped into the front of a somewhat moving city omnibus, which sort of cleaned things out family-wise. Well, no; then there was mom's sister, who was given neither to sin nor the consolation of the bottle. I moved in on her, and my memory of her is slight, excepting I remember still that she did all things dourly: sleeping, eating, working, praying. She dropped dead on the stairs to her apartment, my apartment then, too, on the afternoon of my high school graduation. A terribly middle-European joke, if you ask me.

PETER. Oh, my; oh, my!

JERRY. Oh, your what? But that was a long time ago, and I have no feeling about any of it that I care to admit to myself. Perhaps you can see, though, why good old mom and good old pop are frameless. What's your name? Your first name?

PETER. I'm Peter.

JERRY. I'd forgotten to ask you. I'm Jerry.

PETER (*with a slight, nervous laugh*) Hello, Jerry.

(JERRY *nods his "hello"*)

JERRY. And let's see now; what's the point of having a girl's picture, especially in two frames? I have two picture frames, you remember. I never see the pretty little ladies more than once, and most of them wouldn't be caught in the same room with a camera. It's odd, and I wonder if it's sad.

PETER. The girls?

JERRY. No. I wonder if it's sad that I never see the little ladies more than once. I've never been able to have sex with, or how is it put—make love to anybody more than once. Once, that's it. Oh, wait; for a week and a half, when I was fifteen—and I hang my head in shame that puberty was late—I was a h-o-m-o-s-e-x-u-a-l. I mean I was queer—(*very fast*) queer, queer, queer—with bells ringing, banners snapping in the wind. And for those eleven days, I met at least twice a day with the park superintendent's son—a Greek boy, whose birthday was the same as mine, except he was a year older. I think I was very much in love—maybe just with sex. But that was the jazz of a very special hotel, wasn't it? And now; oh, do I love the little ladies; really, I love them. For about an hour.

PETER. Well, it seems perfectly simple to me . . .

JERRY (*angrily*) Look! Are you going to tell me to get married and have parakeets?

PETER (*angrily*) Forget the parakeets! And stay single if you want to. It's no business of mine. I didn't start this conversation in the . . .

JERRY. All right, all right. I'm sorry. All right? You're not angry?

PETER (*laughing*) No, I'm not angry.

JERRY (*relieved*) Good. · (*Now back to his previous tone*) Interesting that you asked me about the picture frames. I would have thought that you would have asked me about the pornographic playing-cards.

PETER (*with a knowing smile*) Oh, I've seen those cards.

JERRY. That's not the point. (*He laughs*) I suppose when you were a kid you and your pals passed them around, or you had a pack of your own.

PETER. Well, I guess a lot of us did.

JERRY. And you threw them away just before you got married.

PETER. Oh, now; look here. I didn't *need* anything like that when I got older.

JERRY. No?

PETER (*embarrassed*) I'd rather not talk about these things.

JERRY. So? Don't. Besides, I wasn't trying to plumb your post-adolescent sexual life and hand turns; what I wanted to get at is the value difference between pornographic playing-cards when you're a kid, and pornographic playing-cards when you're older. It's that when you're a kid you use the cards as a substitute for a real experience, and when you're older you use real experience as a substitute for the fantasy. But I imagine you'd rather hear about what happened at the Zoo.

PETER (*enthusiastically*) Oh, yes: the Zoo. (*Awkwardly*) That is—if you . . .

JERRY. Let me tell you about why I went—well, let me

tell you some things. I've told you about the fourth floor of the rooming house where I live. I think the rooms are better as you go down, floor by floor. I guess they are; I don't know. I don't know any of the people on the third and second floors. Oh, wait! I do know that there's a lady living on the third floor, in the front. I know because she cries all the time. Whenever I go out or come back in, whenever I pass her door, I always hear her crying, muffled but—very determined. Very determined indeed. But the one I'm getting to, and all about the dog, is the landlady. I don't like to use words that are too harsh in describing people. I don't like to. But the landlady is a fat, ugly, mean, stupid, unwashed, misanthropic, cheap, drunken bag of garbage. And you may have noticed that I very seldom use profanity, so I can't describe her as well as I might.

PETER. You describe her—vividly.

JERRY. Well, thanks. Anyway, she has a dog and I will tell you about the dog, and she and her dog are the gate-keepers of my dwelling. The woman is bad enough; she leans around in the entrance hall, spying to see that I don't bring in things or people, and when she's had her mid-afternoon pint of lemon-flavoured gin she always stops me in the hall, and grabs ahold of my coat or my arm, and she presses her disgusting body up against me to keep me in a corner so she can talk to me. The smell of her body and her breath—you can imagine it—and somewhere, somewhere in the back of that pea-sized brain of hers, an organ developed just enough to let her eat, drink, and emit, she has some foul parody of sexual desire. And I, Peter, I am the object of her sweaty lust.

PETER. That's disgusting. That's—horrible.

JERRY. But I have found a way to keep her off. When she talks to me, when she presses herself to my body and mumbles about her room and how I should come there, I merely say: "But, love; wasn't yesterday enough for you, and the day before?" Then she puzzles, she makes slits of her tiny eyes, she sways a little, and then, Peter—and it is at this moment that I think I might be doing some good in that tormented house—a simple-minded smile begins to form on her unthinkable face, and she giggles and groans as she thinks about yesterday and the day before; as she believes and relives what never happened. Then, she motions to that black monster of a dog she has, and she goes back to her room. And I am safe until our next meeting.

PETER. It's so—unthinkable. I find it hard to believe that people such as that really *are*.

JERRY (*lightly mocking*) It's for reading about, isn't it?

PETER (*seriously*) Yes.

JERRY. And fact is better left to fiction. You're right, Peter. Well, what I have been meaning to tell you about is the dog; I shall now.

PETER (*nervously*) Oh, yes; the dog.

JERRY. Don't go. You're not thinking of going, are you?

PETER. Well—no, I don't think so.

JERRY (*as if to a child*) Because after I tell you about the dog, do you know what then? Then—then I'll tell you about what happened at the Zoo.

PETER (*laughing faintly*) You're—you're full of stories, aren't you?

JERRY. You don't *have* to listen. Nobody is holding you here; remember that. Keep that in your mind.

PETER (*irritably*) I know that.

JERRY. You do? Good.

(*The following long speech should be done with a great deal of action, to achieve a hypnotic effect on* PETER, *and on the audience, too. Some specific actions have been suggested, but the director and the actor playing* JERRY *might best work it out for themselves*)

All right! (*As if reading from a huge billboard*) "The Story of Jerry and the Dog." (*Natural again*) What I am going to tell you has something to do with how sometimes it's necessary to go a long distance out of the way in order to come back a short distance correctly; or, maybe I only think that it has something to do with that. But, it's why I went to the Zoo today, and why I walked north—northerly rather—until I came here. All right. The dog, I think I told you, is a black monster of a beast: an oversized head, tiny, tiny ears, and eyes—bloodshot, infected maybe; and a body you can see the ribs through the skin. The dog is black, all black; all black except for the bloodshot eyes, and —yes—and an open sore on its—*right* forepaw; that is red, too. And, oh, yes; the poor monster, and I do believe it's an old dog—it's certainly a misused one. And—what else —oh, yes; there's a grey-yellow-white colour, too, when he bares his fangs. Like this. (*He demonstrates*) Grrrrrrr! Which is what he did when he saw me for the first time— the day I moved in. I worried about that animal the very first minute I met him. Now, animals don't take to me like St Francis had birds hanging off him all the time. What I mean is: animals are indifferent to me—like people—(*he smiles slightly*) most of the time. But this dog wasn't in-different. From the very beginning he'd snarl, and then go for me, to get one of my legs. Not that he was rabid, you know; he was a stumbly dog, but he wasn't half-assed, either. It was a good, stumbly run; but I always got away. He got a piece of my trouser leg, look, you can see right here, where it's mended; he got that the second day I lived there; but I kicked free and got upstairs fast, so that was that. (*Puzzled*) I still don't know to this day how the other roomers manage it, but you know what I *think:* I think it had to do only with me. Cozy. So. Anyway, this went on for over a week, whenever I came in; but never when I went out. That's funny. Or, it *was* funny. I could pack up and live in the street for all the dog cared. Well, I thought about it up in my room one day, one of the times after I'd bolted upstairs, and I made up my mind. I decided: "First, I'll kill the dog with kindness, and if that doesn't work—I'll just kill him."

(PETER *winces*)

Don't react, Peter; just listen. So, the next day I went out and bought a bag of hamburgers, medium rare, no catsup, no onion; and on the way home I threw away all the rolls and kept just the meat. When I got back to the rooming-house, the dog was waiting for me. I half-opened the door that led into the entrance hall, and there he was; waiting for me. It figured. I went in, very cautiously, and I had the hamburgers, you remember; I opened the

bag, and I set the meat down about twelve feet from where
the dog was snarling at me. Like so! He snarled; stopped
snarling; sniffed; moved slowly; then faster; then faster
towards the meat. Well, when he got to it he stopped, and
he looked at me. I smiled; but tentatively, you understand.
He turned his face back to the hamburgers, smelled, sniffed
some more, and then—*Rrraaaagggghhhh*, like that—he tore
into them. It was as if he had never eaten anything in his
life before, except like garbage. Which might very well have
been the truth. I don't think the landlady ever eats anything but garbage. But. He ate all the hamburgers,
almost all at once, making sounds in his throat like a woman.
Then, when he'd finished the meat, the hamburger, and
tried to eat the paper, too, he sat down and smiled. I think
he smiled; I know cats do. It was a very gratifying few
moments. Then, *bam*, he snarled and made for me again.
He didn't get me this time, either. So, I got upstairs, and
I lay down on my bed and started to think about the dog
again. To be truthful, I was offended, and I was damn mad,
too. It was six perfectly good hamburgers with not enough
pork in them to make it disgusting. I was offended. But,
after a while, I decided to try it for a few more days. If you
think about it, this dog had what amounted to an antipathy
towards me; really. And, I wondered if I mightn't over-
come this antipathy. So, I tried it for five more days, but
it was always the same: snarl, sniff; move; faster; stare;
gobble; *raaggghhh;* smile; snarl; *bam*. Well, now; by this
time Columbus Avenue was strewn with hamburger rolls
and I was less offended than disgusted. So, I decided to
kill the dog.

(PETER *raises a hand in protest*)

Oh, don't be so alarmed, Peter; I didn't succeed. The day
I tried to kill the dog I bought only one hamburger and
what I thought was a murderous portion of rat poison.
When I bought the hamburger I asked the man not to
bother with the roll, all I wanted was the meat. I expected
some reaction from him, like: "We don't sell no hamburgers
without rolls," or, "Wha'd'ya wanna do, eat it out'a ya
hands?" But no, he smiled benignly, wrapped up the

hamburger in waxed paper, and said: "A bite for ya pussy-cat?" I wanted to say, "No, not really; it's part of a plan to poison a dog I know." But, you can't say, "A dog I know" without sounding funny, so I said, a little too loud, I'm afraid, and too formally: *"Yes, a bite for my pussy-cat."* People looked up. It always happens when I try to simplify things; people look up. But that's neither hither nor thither. So. On my way back to the rooming-house, I kneaded the hamburger and the rat poison together between my hands, at that point feeling as much sadness as disgust. I opened the door to the entrance hall, and there the monster was, waiting to take the offering and then jump me. Poor bastard; he never learned that the moment he took to smile before he went for me, gave me time enough to get out of range. *But,* there he was; waiting. I put the poison patty down, moved towards the stairs and watched. The poor animal gobbled the food down as usual, smiled, which made me almost sick, and then, *bam.* But, I sprinted up the stairs, as usual, and the dog didn't get me, as usual. *And it came to pass that the beast was deathly ill.* I knew this because he no longer attended me, and because the land-lady sobered up. She stopped me in the hall the same even-ing of the attempted murder and confided the information that God had struck her puppy-dog a surely fatal blow. She had forgotten her bewildered lust, and her eyes were wide open for the first time. They looked like the dog's eyes. She snivelled and implored me to pray for the animal. I wanted to say to her: "Madam, I have myself to pray for, the coloured queen, the Puerto Rican family, the person in the front room whom I've never seen, the woman who cries deliberately behind her closed door, and the rest of the people in all rooming-houses, everywhere; besides, madam, I don't understand how to pray." But—to simplify things—I told her I would pray. She looked up. She said that I was a liar, and that I probably wanted the dog to die. I told her, and there was so much truth here, that I didn't want the dog to die. I didn't, and not just because I'd poisoned him. I'm afraid that I must tell you I wanted the dog to live so that I could see what our new relationship might come to.

(PETER *indicates his increasing displeasure and slowly growing antagonism*)

Please understand, Peter, that sort of thing is important. You must believe me, it *is* important. We have to know the effect of our actions. (*He sighs deeply*) Well, anyway; the dog recovered. I have no idea why, unless he was a descendant of the puppy that guarded the gates of hell or some such resort. I'm not up on my mythology. (*He pronounces the word myth-o-logy*) Are you?

(PETER *sets to thinking*)

At any rate, and you've missed the eight-thousand-dollar question, Peter; at any rate, the dog recovered his health and the landlady recovered her thirst, in no way altered by the bow-wow's deliverance. When I came home from a movie that was playing on Forty-second Street, a movie I'd seen, or one that was very much like one or several I'd seen, after the landlady told me puppykins was better, I was so hoping for the dog to be waiting for me. I was—well, how would you put it—enticed—fascinated—no, I don't think so—heart-shatteringly anxious, that's it; I was heart-shatteringly anxious to confront my friend again.

(PETER *reacts scoffingly*)

Yes, Peter; friend. That's the only word for it. I was heart-shatteringly *et cetera* to confront my doggy friend again. I came in the door and advanced unafraid, to the centre of the entrance hall. The beast was there—looking at me. And, you know, he looked better for his scrape with the never-mind. I stopped; I looked at him; he looked at me. I think—I think we stayed a long time that way—still, stone-statue—just looking at one another. I looked more into his face than he looked into mine. I mean, I can concentrate longer at looking into a dog's face than a dog can concentrate at looking into mine, or into anybody else's face, for that matter. But during that twenty seconds or two hours that we looked into each other's faces, we made contact. Now, here is what I had wanted to happen: I loved the dog now, and I wanted him to love me. I had tried to love, and I had tried to kill, and both had been unsuccessful by themselves. I hoped—and I don't really know why I expected the dog to understand anything, much less my motivations—I hoped that the dog would understand.

(PETER *seems to be hypnotized*)

It's just—it's just that—(*he is abnormally tense, now*) it's just that if you can't deal with people, you have to make a start somewhere. *With animals.* (*Much faster now, and like a conspirator*) Don't you see? A person has to have some way of dealing with *something.* If not with people—if not with people—*something.* With a bed, with a cockroach, with a mirror—no, that's too hard, that's one of the last steps. With a cockroach, with a—with a—with a carpet, a roll of toilet paper—no, not that, either—that's a mirror, too; always check bleeding. You see how hard it is to find things? With a street corner, and too many lights, all colours reflecting on the oily-wet streets—with a wisp of smoke, a wisp—of smoke—with—with pornographic playing-cards, with a strong-box—*without a lock*—with love, with vomiting, with crying, with fury because the pretty little ladies aren't pretty little ladies, with making money with your body which is an act of love and I could prove it, with howling because you're alive; with God. How about that? With God who is a coloured queen who wears a kimono and plucks his eyebrows, who is a woman who cries with determination behind her closed door—with God, who, I'm told, turned his back on the whole thing some time ago—with—some day, with people. (*He sighs the next word heavily*) People. With an idea; a concept. And where better, where ever better in this humiliating excuse for a jail, where better to communicate one single, simple-minded idea than in the entrance hall? Where? It would be *a start!* Where better to make a beginning—to understand and just possibly to be understood—a beginning of an understanding, than with—(*he seems to fall into almost grotesque fatigue*) than with *a dog.* Just that; a dog.

(*There is a silence*)

(*Wearily*) A dog. It seemed like a perfectly sensible idea.

Man is a dog's best friend, remember. So: the dog and I looked at each other. I longer than the dog. And what I saw then has been the same ever since. Whenever the dog and I see each other we both stop where we are. We regard each other with a mixture of sadness and suspicion, and then we feign indifference. We walk past each other safely; we have an understanding. It's very sad, but you'll have to admit that it is an understanding. We had made many attempts at contact, and we had failed. The dog has returned to garbage, and I to solitary but free passage. I have not returned. I mean to say, I have *gained* solitary free passage, if that much further loss can be said to be gain. I have learned that neither kindness nor cruelty by themselves, independent of each other, creates any effect beyond themselves; and I have learned that the two combined together, at the same time, are the teaching emotion. And what is gained is loss. And what has been the result: the dog and I have attained a compromise; more of a bargain, really. We neither love nor hurt because we do not try to reach each other. And, *was* trying to feed the dog an act of love? And, perhaps, was the dog's attempt to bite me *not* an act of love? If we can so misunderstand, well, then, why have we invented the word love in the first place?

(*There is a silence*)

(*He moves to Peter's bench and sits beside him. This is the first time he has sat during the play*) The Story of Jerry and the Dog: the end.

(PETER *is silent*)

Well, Peter? (*He is suddenly cheerful*) Well, Peter? Do you think I could sell that story to the *Readers' Digest* and make a couple of hundred bucks for *The Most Unforgettable Character I've Ever Met?* (*He is animated*)

(PETER *is disturbed*)

Oh, come on now, Peter; tell me what you think?

PETER (*numb*) I—I don't understand what—I don't think I . . . (*Almost tearfully*) Why did you tell me all of this?

JERRY. Why not?

PETER. *I don't understand!*

JERRY (*furious, but whispering*) That's a lie.

PETER. No. No, it's not.

JERRY (*quietly*) I tried to explain it to you as I went along. I went slowly; it all has to do with . . .

PETER. *I don't want to hear any more.* I don't understand you, or your landlady, or her dog . . .

JERRY. *Her* dog! I thought it was my . . . No. No, you're right. It *is* her dog. (*He looks intently at Peter and shakes his head*) I don't know what I was thinking about; of course you don't understand. (*In a monotone. Wearily*) I don't live in your block; I'm not married with two parakeets, or whatever your set-up is. I am a *permanent transient,* and my home is the sickening rooming-house on the West Side of New York City, which is the greatest city in the world. Amen.

PETER. I'm—I'm sorry; I didn't mean to . . .

JERRY. Forget it. I suppose you don't quite know what to make of me, eh?

PETER (*jokingly*) We get all kinds in publishing. (*He chuckles*)

JERRY. You're a funny man. (*He forces a laugh*) You know that? You're a very—a richly comic person.

PETER (*modestly, but amused*) Oh, now, not really. (*He chuckles*)

JERRY. Peter, do I annoy you, or confuse you?

PETER (*lightly*) Well, I must confess that this wasn't the kind of afternoon I'd anticipated.

JERRY. You mean, I'm not the gentleman you were expecting.

PETER. I wasn't expecting anybody.

JERRY. No, I don't imagine you were. But I'm here, and I'm not leaving.

PETER (*consulting his watch*) Well, you may not be, but I must be getting home soon.

JERRY. Oh, come on; stay a while longer.

PETER. I really should get home; you see . . .

(JERRY *tickles Peter's ribs with his fingers*)

JERRY. Oh, come on.

(PETER *is very ticklish. As* JERRY *continues to tickle him his voice becomes falsetto*)

PETER. No, I . . . *Ohhhhh!* Don't do that. Stop. Stop. Ohhh, no, no.

JERRY. Oh, come on. (*He continues tickling Peter*)

PETER. Oh, hee, hee, hee. I must go. I . . . Hee, hee, hee. After all . . . Stop, stop. Hee, hee, hee. After all, the parakeets will be getting dinner ready soon. Hee, hee. And the cats are setting the table. Stop, stop. And, and— (*he is beside himself now*) and we're having . . . Hee, hee— uh—ho, ho, ho.

(JERRY *stops tickling Peter, but the combination of the tickling and his own mad whimsy has* PETER *laughing almost hysterically. As his laughter continues, then subsides,* JERRY *watches him, with a curious fixed smile*)

JERRY. Peter?

PETER. Oh, ha, ha, ha, ha, ha. What? What?

JERRY. Listen, now.

PETER. Oh, ho, ho. What—what is it, Jerry? Oh, my!

JERRY (*mysteriously*) Peter, do you want to know what happened at the Zoo?

PETER. Ah, ha, ha. The what? Oh, yes; the Zoo. Oh, ho, ho. Well, I had my own zoo there for a moment, with —hee, hee, the parakeets getting dinner ready, and the— ha, ha, whatever it was, the . . .

JERRY (*calmly*) Yes, that was very funny, Peter. I wouldn't have expected it. But do you want to hear about what happened at the Zoo or not?

PETER. Yes. Yes, by all means; tell me what happened at the Zoo. Oh, my. I don't know what happened to me.

JERRY. Now I'll let you in on what happened at the Zoo; but first, I should tell you why I went to the Zoo. I went to the Zoo to find out more about the way people exist with animals, and the way animals exist with each other, and with people, too. It probably wasn't a fair test, what with everyone separated by bars from everyone else, the animals for the most part from each other, and always the people from the animals. But if it's a Zoo, that's the way it is. (*He pokes Peter on the arm*) Move over.

PETER (*friendly*) I'm sorry, haven't you enough room? (*He shifts a little*)

JERRY (*smiling slightly*) Well, all the animals are there, and all the people are there, and it's Sunday and all the children are there. (*He pokes Peter*) Move over.

PETER (*patiently and still friendly*) All right.

(PETER *moves some more and* JERRY *has all the room he might need*)

JERRY. And it's a hot day, so all the stench is there, too, and all the balloon sellers, and all the ice-cream sellers, and all the seals are barking, and all the birds are screaming. (*He pokes Peter harder*) Move over.

PETER (*beginning to be annoyed*) Look here, you have more than enough room. (*He moves and is now fairly cramped at one end of the bench*)

JERRY. And I am, there, and it's feeding time at the lions' house, and the lion-keeper comes into the lion cage, one of the lion cages, to feed one of the lions. (*He punches Peter on the arm, annoyed*) *Move over!*

PETER (*very annoyed*) I can't move over any more, and stop hitting me. What's the matter with you?

JERRY. Do you want to hear the story? (*He punches Peter's arm*)

PETER (*flabbergasted*) I'm not so sure. I certainly don't want to be punched in the arm.

JERRY (*punching Peter's arm*) Like that?

PETER. Stop it! What's the matter with you?

JERRY. I'm crazy, you bastard.

PETER. That isn't funny.

JERRY. Listen to me, Peter. I want this bench. You go sit on the bench over there, and if you're good I'll tell you the rest of the story.

PETER (*flustered*) But—whatever for? What *is* the matter with you? Besides, I see no reason why I should give up this bench. I sit on this bench almost every Sunday afternoon, in good weather. It's secluded here; there's never anyone sitting here, so I have it all to myself.

JERRY (*softly*) Get off this bench, Peter; I want it.

PETER (*almost whining*) No.

JERRY. I said I want this bench, and I'm going to have it. Now, get over there.

PETER. People can't have everything they want. You should know that; it's a rule; people can have some of the things they want, but they can't have everything.

(JERRY *laughs*)

JERRY. Imbecile! You're slow-witted!

PETER. Stop that!

JERRY. You're a vegetable. Go lie down on the ground.

PETER (*intense*) Now *you* listen to me. I've put up with you all afternoon . . .

JERRY. Not really.

PETER. *Long enough.* I've put up with you long enough. I've listened to you because you seemed—well, because I thought you wanted to talk to somebody.

JERRY. You put things well; economically, and, yet . . . Oh, what is the word I want to put justice to your . . . You make me sick—get off here and give me my bench.

PETER. *My bench.*

(JERRY *pushes Peter almost, but not quite off the bench*)

JERRY. Get out of my sight.

PETER (*regaining his position*) God da-mn you. That's enough! I've had enough of you. I will not give up this bench; you can't have it, and that's that. Now, go away.

(JERRY *snorts but does not move*)

Go away, I said.

(JERRY *does not move*)

Get away from here. If you don't move on . . . You're a bum—that's what you are. If you don't move on, I'll get a policeman here and make you go.

(JERRY *laughs*)

I warn you, I'll call a policeman.

JERRY (*softly*) You won't find a policeman around here;

they're all over on the west side of the park chasing fairies down from the trees or out of the bushes. That's all they do. That's their function. So scream your head off; it won't do you any good.

PETER (*shouting*) Police! I warn you, I'll have you arrested. (*He shouts*) Police! (*He pauses*) I said *Police!* (*He pauses*) I feel ridiculous.

JERRY. You look ridiculous: a grown man screaming for the police on a bright Sunday afternoon in the park with nobody harming you. If a policeman *did* fill his quota and come sludging over this way he'd probably take you in as a nut.

PETER (*with disgust and impotence*) Great God, I just came here to read, and now you want me to give up the bench. You're mad.

JERRY. Hey, I got news for you, as they say. I'm on your precious bench, and you're never going to have it for yourself again.

PETER (*furiously*) Look, you; get off my bench. I don't care if it makes any sense or not. I want this bench to myself; I want you *off it*.

JERRY (*mocking*) Aw—look who's mad.

PETER. *Get out!*

JERRY. No.

PETER. *I warn you.*

JERRY. Do you know how ridiculous you look *now?*

PETER (*his fury and self-consciousness have possessed him*) It doesn't matter. (*He is almost crying*) *Get away from my bench.*

JERRY. Why? You have everything in the world you want; you've told me about your home, and your family, and *your own* little Zoo. You have everything, and now you want this bench. Are these the things men fight for? Tell me, Peter, is this bench, this iron and this wood, is this your honour? Is this the thing in the world you'd fight for? Can you think of anything more absurd?

PETER. Absurd? Look, I'm not going to talk to you about honour, or even try to explain it to you. Besides, it isn't a question of honour; but even if it were, you wouldn't understand.

JERRY (*contemptuously*) You don't even know what you're saying, do you? This is probably the first time in your life you've had anything more trying to face than changing your cats' toilet box. Stupid! Don't you have any idea, not even the slightest, what other people *need?*

PETER. Oh, boy, listen to you; well, you don't need this bench. That's for sure.

JERRY. Yes; yes, I do.

PETER (*quivering*) I've come here for years; I have hours of great pleasure, great satisfaction, right here. And that's important to a man. I'm a responsible person, and I'm a *grown-up*. This is my bench, and you have no right to take it away from me.

JERRY. Fight for it, then. Defend yourself; defend your bench.

PETER. You've *pushed* me to it. Get up and fight.

JERRY. Like a man?

PETER. Yes, like a man, if you insist on mocking me even further.

JERRY. I'll have to give you credit for one thing: you *are* a vegetable, and a slight near-sighted one, I think——

PETER. *That's enough!*

JERRY. —but, you know, as they say on TV all the time —you know—and I mean this, Peter, you have a certain dignity; it surprises me.

PETER. *Stop!*

JERRY (*rising lazily*) Very well, Peter, we'll battle for the bench, but we're not evenly matched. (*He takes out an ugly-looking knife and flicks it open*)

PETER (*suddenly awakening to the reality of the situation*) You *are* mad! You're stark raving mad! *You're going to kill me!*

(*Before* PETER *has time to think what to do,* JERRY *tosses the knife at Peter's feet*)

JERRY. There you go. Pick it up. You have the knife and we'll be more evenly matched.

PETER (*horrified*) No!

(JERRY *grabs Peter by the collar.* PETER *rises. Their faces almost touch*)

JERRY. Now, you pick up that knife and you fight with me. You fight for your self-respect; you fight for that god-damned bench.

PETER (*struggling*) No! Let—let go of me! (*He yells*) He-help!

JERRY. You fight, you miserable bastard. (*He slaps Peter on each "fight"*) Fight for that bench; fight for your para-keets; fight for your cats, fight for your two daughters; fight for your wife; fight for your manhood, you pathetic little vegetable. (*He spits in Peter's face*) You couldn't even get your wife with a male child.

PETER (*breaking away; enraged*) It's a matter of genetics, not manhood, you—you monster. (*He darts down, picks up the knife and backs away a little, breathing heavily*) I'll give you one last chance; get out of here and leave me alone. (*He holds the knife with a firm arm, but far in front of him, not to attack, but to defend*)

JERRY (*sighing heavily*) So be it! (*With a rush he charges Peter and impales himself on the knife*)

(*For just a moment there is complete silence. JERRY impaled on the knife at the end of PETER's still firm arm. Then PETER screams and pulls away, leaving the knife in Jerry. JERRY is motionless for a moment, then he, too, screams, sounding like an infuriated and fatally wounded animal. With the knife in him, he stumbles back to the bench they vacated. He crumbles there, sitting facing Peter, his eyes wide in agony, his mouth open*)

PETER (*whispering*) Oh, my God; oh, my God; oh, my God . . . (*He repeats these words many times, very rapidly*)

(*JERRY is dying, but now his expression seems to change. His features relax, and while his voice varies, sometimes wrenched with pain, for the most part he seems removed from his dying*)

JERRY (*smiling*) Thank you, Peter. I mean that, now; thank you very much.

(*PETER's mouth drops open. He cannot move, he is trans-fixed*)

Oh, Peter, I was so afraid I'd drive you away. (*He laughs as best he can*) You don't know how afraid I was you'd go away and leave me. And now I'll tell you what happened at the Zoo. I think—I think this is what happened at the Zoo—I think. I think that while I was at the Zoo I decided that I would walk north—northerly, rather—until I found you—or somebody—and I decided that I would talk to you —I would tell you things—and things that I would tell you would . . . Well, here we are. You see? Here we *are*. But—I don't know—could I have planned all this? No— no, no, I couldn't have. But I think I did. And now I've told you what you wanted to know, haven't I? And now you know all about what happened at the Zoo. And now you know what you'll see in your TV, and the face I told you about—you remember—the face I told you about—my face, the face you see right now. Peter—Peter? Peter—thank you. I came unto you—(*he laughs, so faintly*) and you have comforted me. Dear Peter.

PETER (*almost fainting*) Oh, my God!

JERRY. You'd better go now. Somebody might come by, and you don't want to be here when anyone comes.

(PETER *does not move and begins to weep*)

PETER. Oh, my God; oh, my God!

JERRY (*most faintly now, he is very near death*) You won't be coming back here any more, Peter; you've been dispossessed. You've lost your bench, but you've defended your honour. And, Peter, I'll tell you something now; you're not really a vegetable; it's all right, you're an animal. You're an animal, too. But you'd better hurry now, Peter. Hurry, you'd better go—see? (*He takes out his handkerchief and with great effort and pain wipes the knife handle clean of fingerprints*) Hurry away, Peter.

(PETER *turns to stagger away*)

Wait—wait, Peter.

(PETER *stops and turns*)

Take your book—book. Right here—beside me—on you bench—my bench, rather. Come—take your book.

(PETER *starts for the book, but retreats*)

Hurry—Peter.

(PETER *rushes to the bench, grabs the book and retreats*)

Very good, Peter—very good. Now—hurry away.

(PETER *hesitates for a moment, then dashes off* L)

Hurry away. (*His eyes close*) Hurry away, your parakeets are making the dinner—the cats—are setting the table . . .
  PETER (*off* L; *a pitiful howl*) Oh, my God!

(JERRY, *his eyes closed, shakes his head*)

  JERRY (*a combination of scornful mimicry and supplication*) Oh —my—God. (*He is dead*)

CURTAIN

FURNITURE AND PROPERTY LIST

"PARK" BACKCLOTH

PARK BENCH   PARK BENCH

On stage: 2 park benches

Personal: PETER: book, horn-rimmed glasses, pipe, handkerchief,
              pouch with tobacco, matches, watch
        JERRY: flick-knife, handkerchief

MADE AND PRINTED IN GREAT BRITAIN BY
BUTLER & TANNER LTD
FROME AND LONDON